Quarto
Knows

Inspiring | Educating | Creating | Entertaining

Brimming with creative inspiration, how-to projects, and useful information to enrich your everyday life, Quarto Knows is a favourite destination for those pursuing their interests and passions. Visit our site and dig deeper with our books into your area of interest: Quarto Creates, Quarto Cooks, Quarto Homes, Quarto Lives, Quarto Drives, Quarto Explores, Quarto Gifts, or Quarto Kids.

First Published as *Menino, Menina* in 2020 by Planeta Tangerina in Lisbon, Portugal.

First published in the US in 2022 by Wide Eyed Editions,
an imprint of The Quarto Group.
100 Cummings Center, Suite 265D, Beverly, MA 01915 USA.
T +1 978-282-9590 F +1 978-283-2742 **www.QuartoKnows.com**

Translated from the original Portuguese by Jay Hulme.

A catalog record for this book is available from the Library of Congress.

ISBN 978-0-7112-6586-8

The illustrations were created with wax crayons and digital tools.
Set in Wiseley

Published by Georgia Amson-Bradshaw
Designed by Sasha Moxon
Edited by Hattie Grylls
Production by Dawn Cameron

Manufactured in Guangdong, China CC102021

9 8 7 6 5 4 3 2 1

MY OWN WAY

JOANA ESTRELA
Adapted by JAY HULME

WIDE EYED EDITIONS

WHAT BRINGS
YOU JOY?

IT'S UP TO YOU.

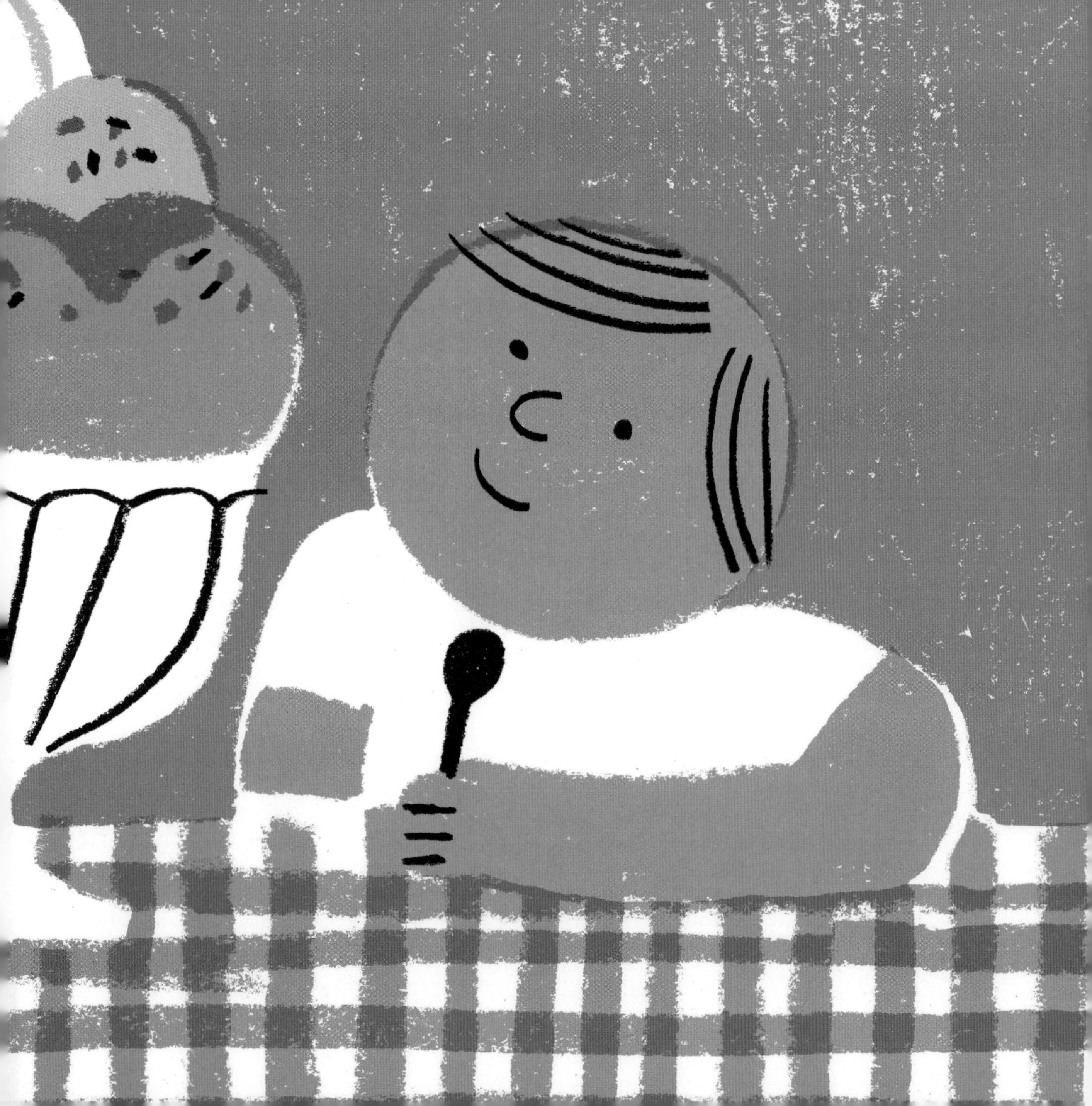

"HOW WILL
YOU DRESS?"

"WHAT WILL YOU PLAY?"

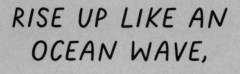

RISE UP LIKE AN
OCEAN WAVE,

BE YOURSELF:
FREE AND BRAVE!

"GIRLFRIEND?
BOYFRIEND?"

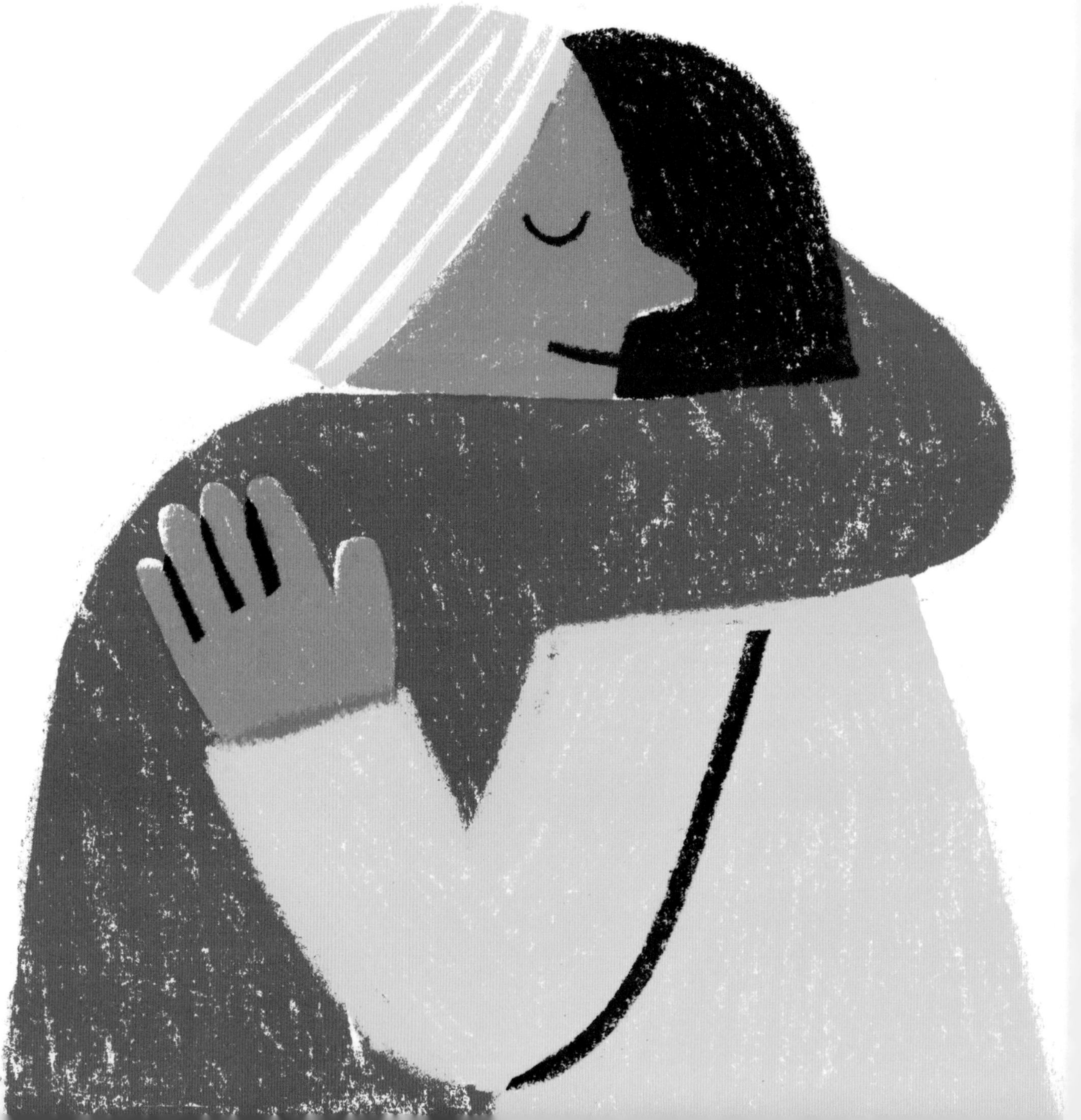

MY GRANDMA USED
TO TELL ME,

"EVERYONE HAS
THEIR OWN WAY."

"YOU CAN
SEE THE
DIFFERENT
FACES,

BUT THE
REST IS
THEIRS
TO SAY."

JUST BE AS KIND
AS YOU CAN.

BOY OR GIRL

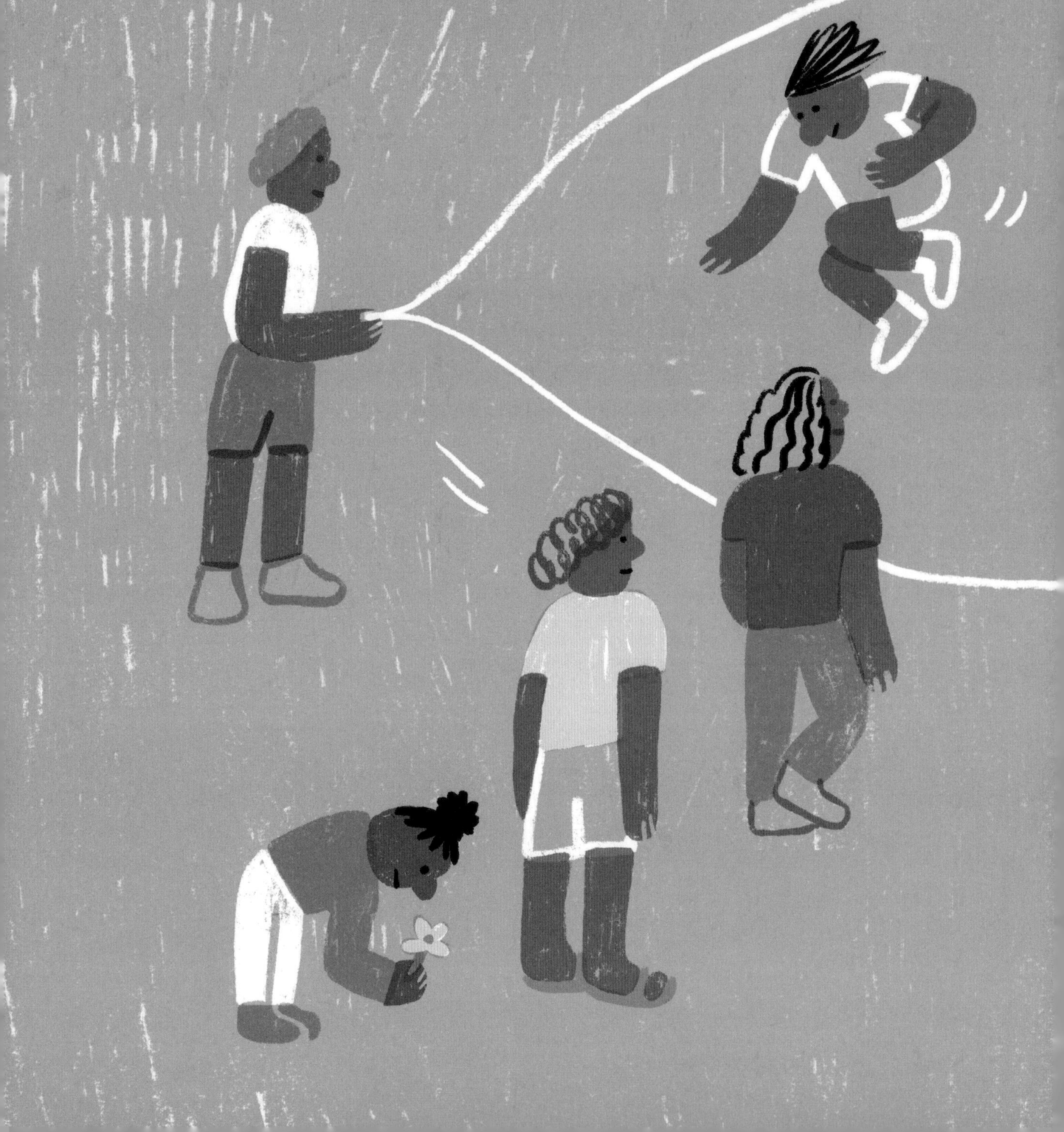

DOESN'T COVER
EVERYONE.

YOU MIGHT BE NONE!

YOUR TRUTH ISN'T HIDDEN
UNDERNEATH YOUR CLOTHES,

YOUR TRUTH IS SOMETHING
ONLY YOU CAN KNOW.

YOU ARE NOT
ONLY A BOY
OR A GIRL.

INSIDE OF YOU
IS A WHOLE
WIDE WORLD!

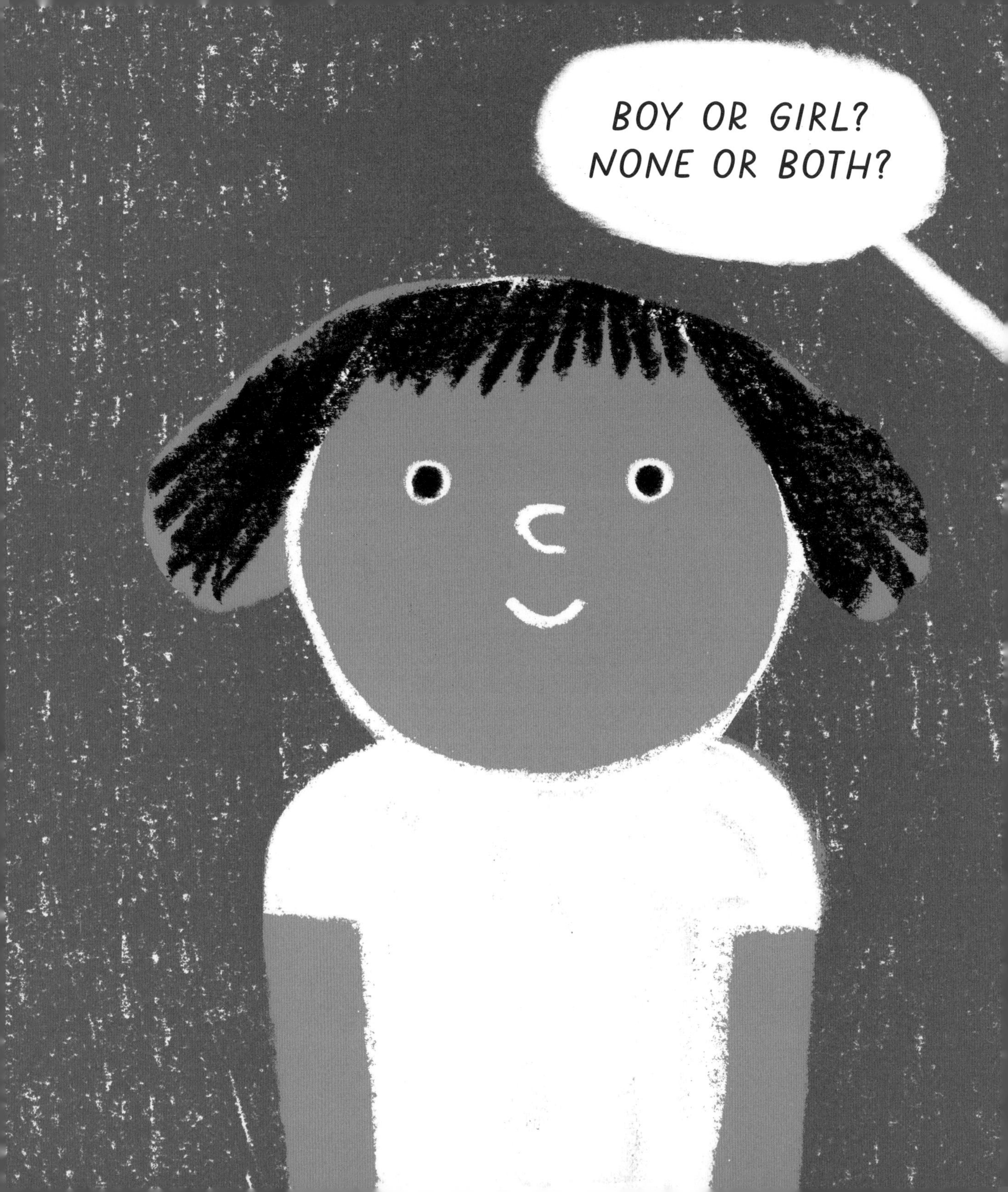
BOY OR GIRL? NONE OR BOTH?

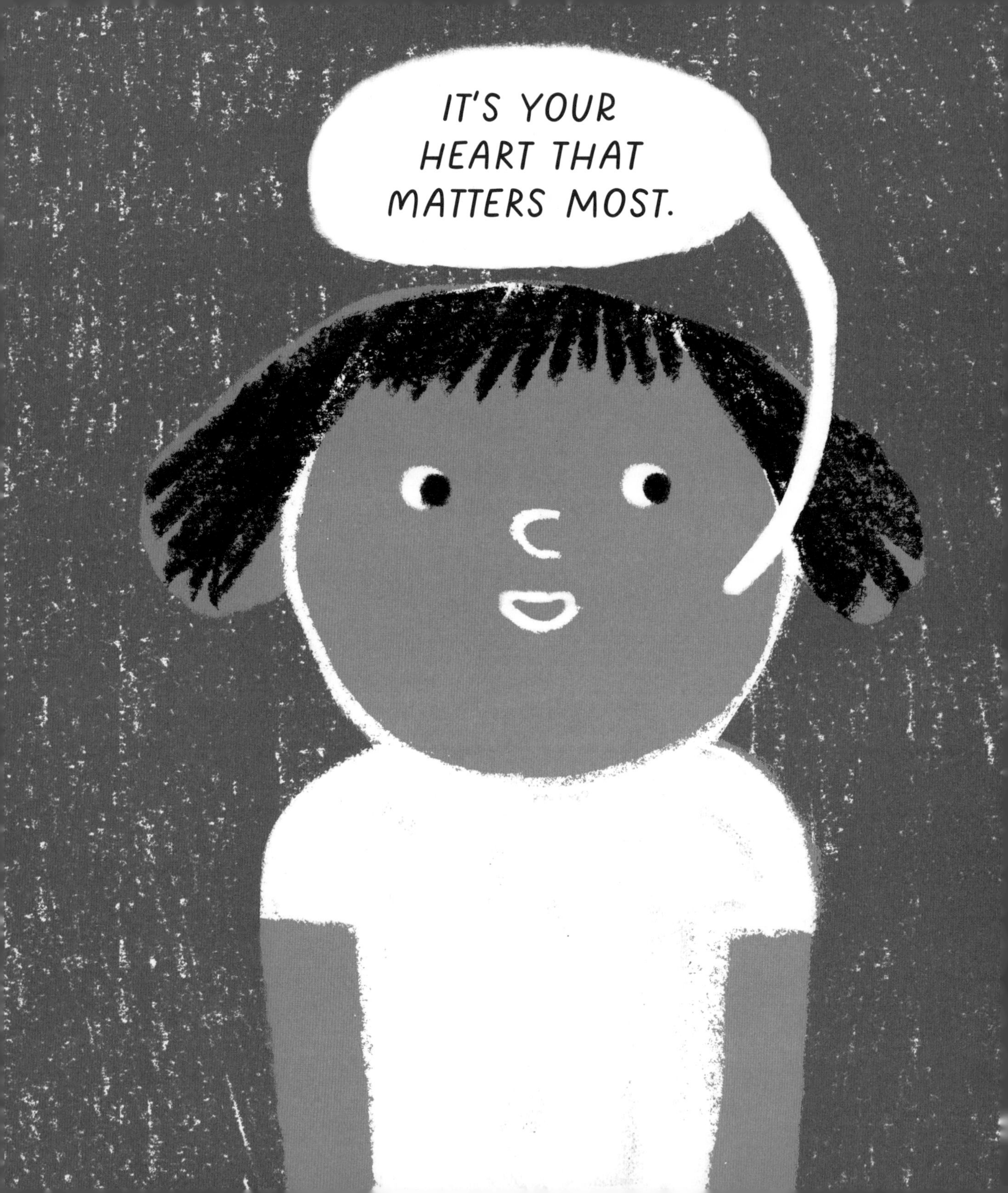
IT'S YOUR HEART THAT MATTERS MOST.

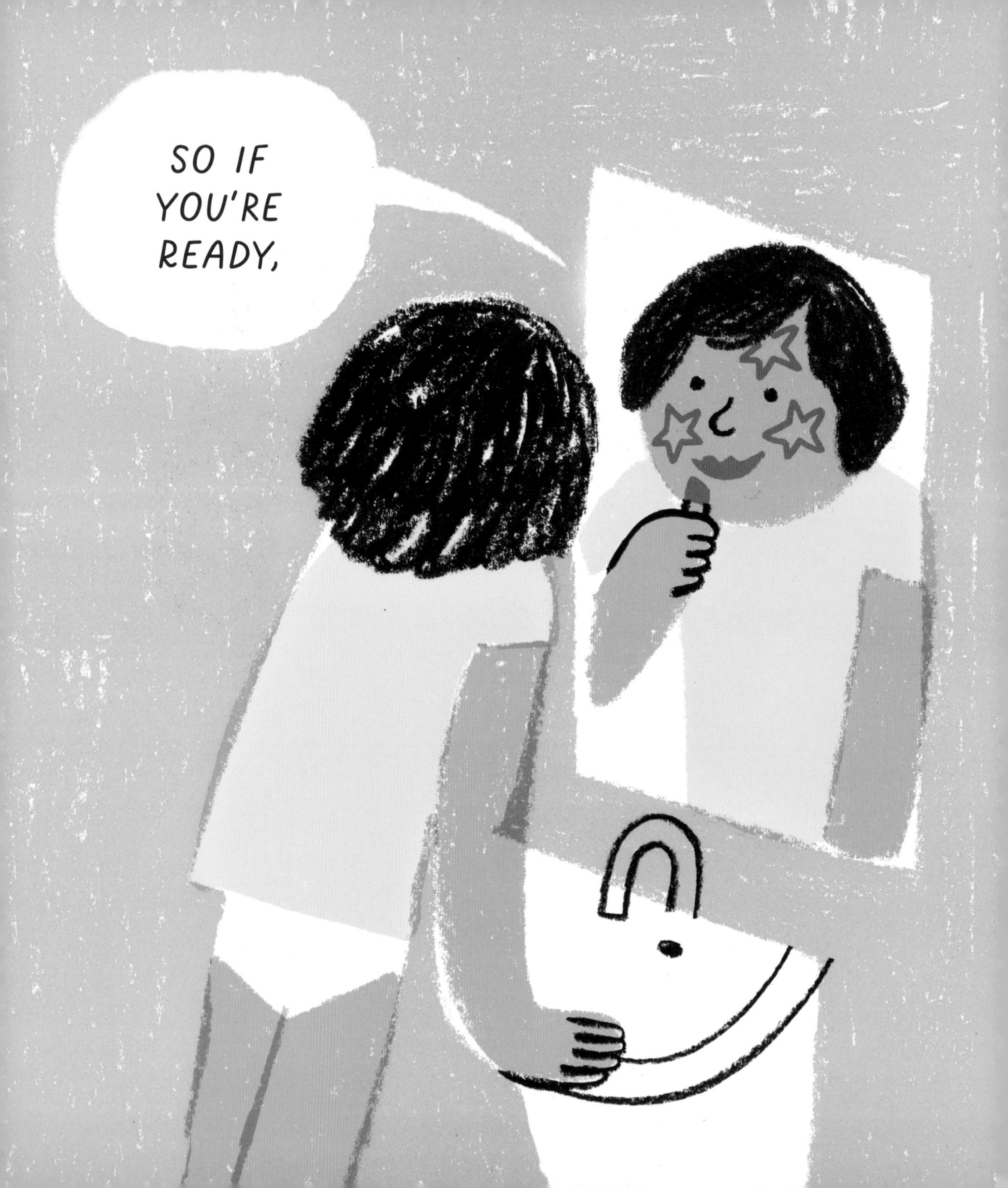
SO IF YOU'RE READY,